Dinosaurs

Written by Emily Bone

Illustrated by Lee Cosgrove

Designed by Zoe Wray

Dinosaurs consultant: Dr. Darren Naish,
University of Southampton

Reading consultant: Alison Kelly

Dinosaurs were creatures that lived millions and millions of years ago.

Some had scaly skin.

Brachiosaurus

Others had feathers.

Citipati

Some had rows of sharp spines.

Pinacosaurus

Others had big, sharp teeth.

Tarbosaurus

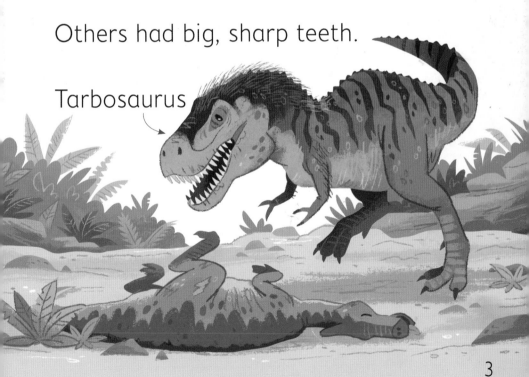

Some dinosaurs were enormous.

Spinosaurus was
almost as long
as two buses.

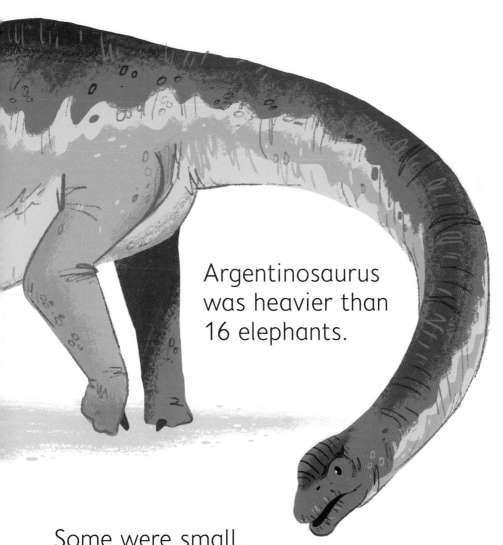

Argentinosaurus
was heavier than
16 elephants.

Some were small.

A microraptor
was the size of
a chicken.

The world was very different when dinosaurs lived. There were lots of dry, hot deserts.

Gobivenator

Protoceratops

There were wide, deep rivers too.

Deinosuchus

Kritosaurus

Lots of places were covered
in huge, thick forests.

Alamosaurus

Many dinosaurs ate plants.

Stegosaurus had a sharp mouth, like a beak. It bit through plant stalks.

Diplodocus had a long neck to reach leaves in trees.

It could stretch out to grab plants too.

9

Some dinosaurs ate meat.

Velociraptor hunted
small animals.

Juramaia

It had very sharp claws. It used its
claws to pin animals to the ground.

Baryonyx caught fish to eat.

It used a big claw on its hand
to spike fish out of the water.

Tyrannosaurus rex was one of the biggest, fiercest dinosaurs.

Lots of
sharp teeth

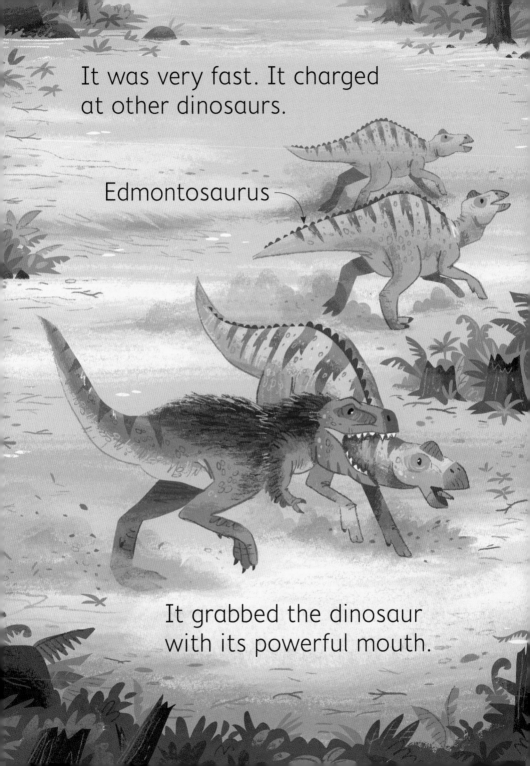

It was very fast. It charged
at other dinosaurs.

Edmontosaurus

It grabbed the dinosaur
with its powerful mouth.

Dinosaurs had different ways to protect themselves.

Ankylosaurus hit other dinosaurs with the club on its tail.

Club

Ankylosaurus

Acheroraptor

Tyrannosaurus rex

Triceratops had a bony frill to protect its neck.

Frill

It stabbed other dinosaurs with its sharp horns.

Baby Triceratops

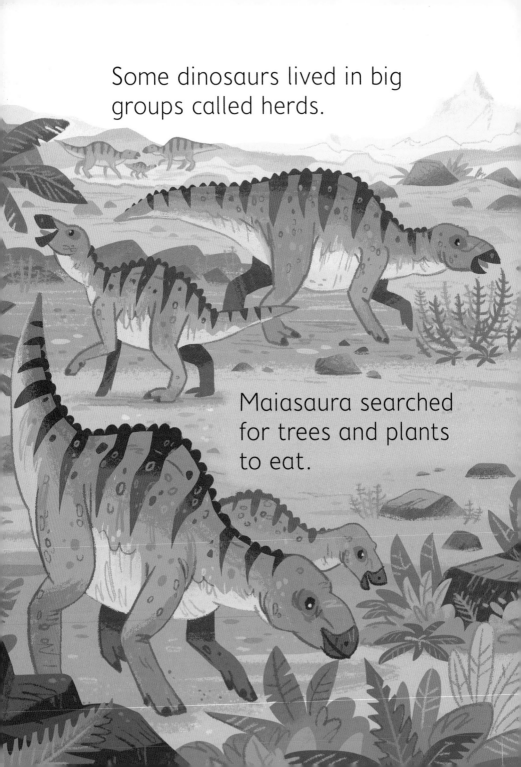

Some dinosaurs lived in big groups called herds.

Maiasaura searched for trees and plants to eat.

Parents looked after their babies.

They scared away
other dinosaurs.

Troodon →

17

Baby dinosaurs hatched out of eggs.

A mother Citipati got ready to lay eggs. She made a nest.

She laid lots of eggs in the nest.

The parents sat on the eggs to keep them warm.

Baby Citipati hatched out of the eggs.

Some parent dinosaurs looked after their babies.

Allosaurus brought food to their babies.

Other babies had to look
after themselves.

Apatosaurus laid eggs. Then they
left the eggs behind.

Babies hatched out. They found
food to eat.

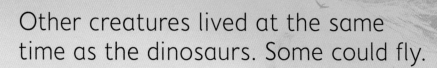

Other creatures lived at the same time as the dinosaurs. Some could fly.

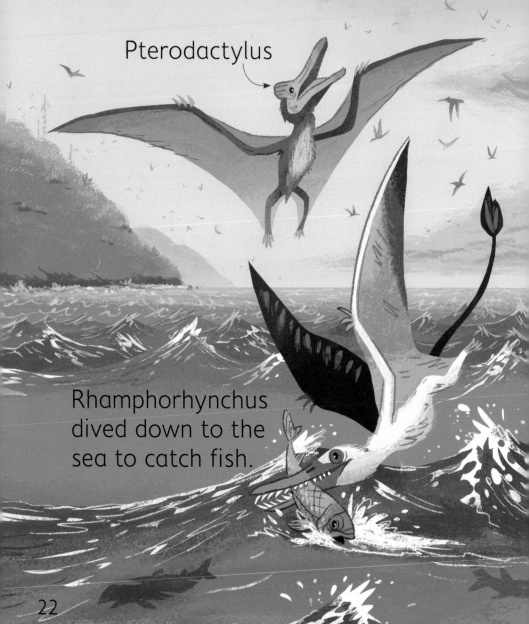

Pterodactylus

Rhamphorhynchus dived down to the sea to catch fish.

Hatzegopteryx was very, very big.
It hunted small dinosaurs.

Young Magyarosaurus

All kinds of different creatures lived under the sea.

Tylosaurus hunted sharks.

Shark

Platecarpus

Ammonites had shells.

Mosasaurus

Large
squid

There were dinosaurs on Earth for millions of years.

One day, a massive rock from space crashed into the Earth.

It probably became cold and dark.
Many plants died.

Plant-eating dinosaurs had nothing
to eat. Slowly they died out.

Meat-eating dinosaurs had nothing
to eat either. They died out too.

Dinosaur remains are called fossils.
They are buried under the ground.

Triceratops fossil

Scientists carefully dig up
dinosaur fossils.

They take the fossils away.
Then they clean off any dirt.

Scientists work out how dinosaur bones fit together.

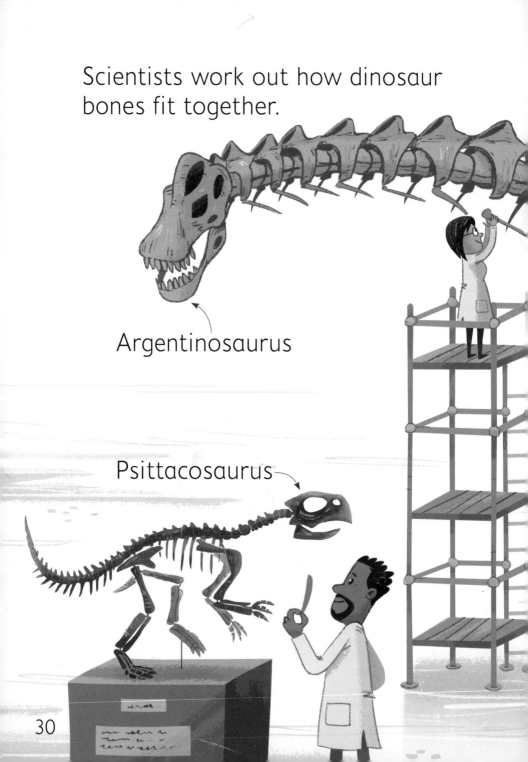

Argentinosaurus

Psittacosaurus

Pterosaur

Velociraptor

Some dinosaurs also left behind huge footprints.

These are Acrocanthosaurus footprints.

Digital retouching by John Russell

First published in 2016 by Usborne Publishing Ltd., Usborne House, 83-85 Saffron Hill, London EC1N 8RT England. www.usborne.com Copyright © 2016 Usborne Publishing Ltd. The name Usborne and the devices 🎈 are Trade Marks of Usborne Publishing Ltd. All rights reserved. U.E. First published in America in 2016.